G000300499

ONE CRIMSON THREAD

Micheal O'Siadhail was born in 1947. He was educated at Clongowes Wood College, Trinity College Dublin, and the University of Oslo. A full-time writer, he was awarded an Irish American Cultural Institute prize for poetry in 1982, and the Marten Toonder Prize for Literature in 1998. His *Collected Poems* was published by Bloodaxe Books in 2013, and his book of essays, *Say but the Word: Poetry as Vision and Voice*, by Hinds Publishing in 2015.

He has been a lecturer at Trinity College Dublin and a professor at the Dublin Institute for Advanced Studies. Among his many academic works are *Learning Irish* (Yale University Press, 1988) and *Modern Irish* (Cambridge University Press, 1989). He now divides his time between Dublin and New York.

Micheal O'Siadhail

ONE CRIMSON THREAD

Mr Fitzpatrick.

With Love

Rosie x

BLOODAXE BOOKS

Copyright © Micheal O'Siadhail 2015

ISBN: 978 1 78037 127 6

First published 2015 by
Bloodaxe Books Ltd,
Eastburn,
South Park,
Hexham,
Northumberland NE46 1BS

www.bloodaxebooks.com
For further information about Bloodaxe titles
please visit our website or write to
the above address for a catalogue.

Supported using public funding by
ARTS COUNCIL
ENGLAND

LEGAL NOTICE

All rights reserved. No part of this book may be
reproduced, stored in a retrieval system, or
transmitted in any form, or by any means, electronic,
mechanical, photocopying, recording or otherwise,
without prior written permission from Bloodaxe Books Ltd.

Requests to publish work from this book
must be sent to Bloodaxe Books Ltd.

Micheal O'Siadhail has asserted his right under
Section 77 of the Copyright, Designs and Patents Act 1988
to be identified as the author of this work.

Cover design: Neil Astley & Pamela Robertson-Pearce.

Printed in Great Britain by Bell & Bain Limited, Glasgow, Scotland, on
acid-free paper sourced from mills with FSC chain of custody certification.

For all who cared for Bríd

ONE CRIMSON THREAD

1

Such trembling is no news; the shuffling gait,
The freeze or wobbled head or winkless look,
All ons and offs that you and I, your mate
Of two score years, absorbed – but how this snuck
Unfairly up on us. I stammer it:
Dementia. A name for you my love?
In such a word do our two lives unknit?
Without your hand, my life's an empty glove.

I ask and ask but do I ask in vain?
Have I received a stone instead of bread,
A nightmare that no waking will relieve?
A sabotage has spread across your brain,
Unravelling our long-ravelled crimson thread.
My Bríd have you begun to take your leave?

2

Should I have seen it coming all along?
Those hints and quirks that now with hindsight seem
Non sequiturs, slight glitches, small things wrong,
Strange angles of approach a touch off-beam.
My sight too lured by memories, too layered,
How could I see with these long-loving eyes
Which take for granted every gift we shared?
My mind declines the grief my heart denies.

We swing and switch between opposing poles:
My stumbling child I lift and clothe and tend,
My elegant hostess to guests we house.
In all our sudden shifts between two roles
My word the word on which you must depend;
Your minder now and still your lovesick spouse.

3

Your body bends to every drag and schlep
To shunt its load along a precipice,
Aware how gravity undoes you step by step.
And all your life you lived in dread of this.
Your father's sister Mary Nancy cracked;
A giddy gene had set her mind askew,
A flawed accessory before the fact...
But now it's Parkinson's that nobbles you.

We shared our youth and prime; this too we'll share.
'Just hold my hand,' you cry. 'Don't let me fall!'
Then: 'Why are you there standing in my space?'
The selfsame time both there and yet not there?
To disengage yet hear your deepest call –
But how to hold and still stand back a pace?

4

Although dependence moans against the grain,
Night after night I hoist you half-asleep
Until my lower back baulks at the strain,
The heave and groan of you my rag-doll heap.
A Gatch bed now where buttons choose the height
So I can floor you lightly on your feet
Or tilt you from discomfort in the night –
A boon for both that is so bittersweet.

Here on my nurse's bunk I rest alone
With you cribbed in and me caged out –
All this to aid you in your sleep and ease;
Re-singled man I summon on my own
Our bedded years of turn and turn about,
Your kneecaps in the hollows of my knees.

5

Your whims for all who know you so bizarre –
Can shifts of mind and mood be really you?
How biochemical our psyches are,
This web of what we are and what we do.
'You're hurting me,' you rail, 'you're far too rough!'
Your helplessness beyond what you can bear
And nothing that I do is deemed enough
So you lash out at me in your despair.

O Lord, I am no blameless upright Job;
Forgive me when I groan and bend until
I think my all too human back will break!
Is this some wager with Old Nick to probe
My steadfastness, to plumb and proof my will
To love you in my love for your love's sake?

6

I find you talking to an absent friend
Or nagged by some imagined bête noire,
Yet loath to play along or condescend
I have to be a human aide-mémoire.
Would it be sometimes kinder to let go,
More gracious maybe not to gainsay you
And settle for a neutral 'Is that so?'
Respecting what for you must seem so true?

Why should I undermine what's undermined
And take you from reality's terrain?
Now gently I explain there's just us two;
Your unseen guests are gremlins in the mind
Suggesting you succumb to their domain.
I can't yet yield and so give up on you.

7

How every day you rise to shower and dress
Hell bent on holding all your poise and worth;
Though zips and buttons cost such strain or stress,
Your style still elegant and down-to-earth.
In suffering more lovely day by day –
Your autumn shades now, even as you pale,
Allow a playful luminance to weigh
A face still found unwanting though you fail.

Such flair and fashion sense! My lover-wife
Of late unfolding sides unseen before,
I glean a strange flirtatious girl-like you,
As though you now lay open all your life;
The more that you depend on me the more
You show me younger years I never knew.

8

Though all who know me warn I look too worn,
I have and hold in sickness or in health.
If I collapse, who'll mind you then? I'm torn
Between a vow and burn-out now by stealth.
We call to see a place for daytime care.
'Dementia we never mention here,'
The head-nurse winks, 'in case we are aware!'
In every *we* an *us* and *them* is clear.

Her charges yet too old and too far gone –
An old man wants your stick and won't let go.
'If it's a help for you,' you say, 'I'll stay.'
We've forms to fill but how can I go on?
We home again though in my gut I know
Our time ahead is numbered day by day.

9

Your concentration slithers notch by notch;
Your mind can't cope with so much giving care –
A weanling from your constant trust and watch,
Alone I choose which thoughts to shun or share.
I need someone I love and am loved by;
I could go first, but now, but if you're the one…
My guilty reveries again reply:
Who'd ever understand as you have done?

Such selfish thoughts are time betrayed –
I feel a distance in your frightened eyes,
A glance of a remove, a hint of drift;
I shouldn't jump ahead but I'm afraid
I'll be some stranger you won't recognise;
Each glimpse of you is now a ransomed gift.

10

'Where did I leave my other leather glove,
My bag, the walking stick, the winter hat?'
Your glasses should be on that shelf above;
You're wasting time in losing this and that.
For months I tried in vain to give advice:
Just put them always in one place you choose;
You mean to do it, manage once or twice
And then forget or make some faint excuse.

Impatient had I wanted all just so?
For you my logic can no longer gel;
The you I want to help I only hound,
Compassion cannot pull against the flow;
I know that no one would have loved so well
If things had run the other way around.

11

Another night in anger you declare
That I'm a hard and heartless bully who
Can hold you in captivity by care,
'A prisoner I now depend on you'.
Though trained to understand and simply say:
'I'm doing all I can, I'll do my best',
Again I buck and, bridling in dismay,
'Stop giving out, for God's sake,' I protest.

Are you that woman I once thought I knew,
My flesh of flesh, sweet bone of bone,
With whom for forty years I've honeymooned?
I can't believe this changeling can be you!
Here is a stranger I have never known.
A worn Samaritan I bind your wound.

12

At twenty, spending your first teacher's pay,
You'd bought fresh flowers to mark your own début
And always since when shopping, that bouquet
You'd bring me saying 'These I've bought for you.'
So many of our roles we switch and swap;
Atop my trolley in the long till queue
The one requisite in my weekly shop
A bunch of yellow roses bought for you.

But look! You've left two on my table-top,
So lone and so alike in every fold,
Two heads there poised in mutual repose,
Though one begins to fade and seems to flop,
Head-low with love its stem still tries to hold
The petal-packed remembrance of a rose.

13

What you discard again you choose to hoard –
From bag to bag you shuffle clothes away;
Each time I pleaded with you, I implored:
'Tomorrow don't undo what's done today.'
But totally engrossed, your thoughts intense,
As prayers counting beads to help them pray;
So thorough and as though it all made sense,
Your need to feel you've still a part to play.

My analogue and yoke-mate in all things,
Such wasted days when spirits might have soared –
Sour Sisyphus's stone was less than this.
I want to lift your tired and damaged wings,
Release you from this looped paralysis,
Once lavish hostess of my house and board.

14

For givers it takes greater trust to take –
Dependence proves for you a bitter cup.
But help I seek I'm seeking for your sake;
Alone I can no longer hold you up.
The townland child you were is chiding me:
'You're telling everybody everything'
Though trying to protect your dignity,
I call on friends, I'm coping on the wing.

As hostess coming so into your own,
Your ease ensuring everyone unwound –
Though those invited I had introduced;
But now you can no longer be alone,
A roster of the faithful rally round,
Those guests you'd hosted coming home to roost.

15

But nightmares dawn a little now and then,
Those times together wholly clear and real;
A weekend's gift when you're yourself again
I wonder can I wake from this ordeal.
You turned up trumps at every turning point
For sixteen years while we held out in hope;
On your advice – yet our decision's joint –
The time has come we can no longer cope.

A sage and long-discerning heart that seems
Intent on proving love is shatterproof
Re-thinks our forty years in thanks and praise.
In age do memories become our dreams?
A home that is no home, an unshared roof,
Which still in hope you name another phase.

16

Throughout your years your chest-close cards well kept –
For all your warmth, your need for privacy;
A borderline nobody overstepped,
A conscious self-surround of dignity.
A loving trust, a whole new letting go
Begins alone with rostered friends I feel
My absence now allows you get to know;
It seems there're things you're daring to reveal.

One tells me once you wept in her embrace
But not because you'll miss your memory,
Because you pity me – your cries confide –
That day you'll neither know my name nor face.
Much more than for yourself you fear for me;
So you! my lifelong Bríd, my selfless bride.

17

At bedtime now a battle to undress,
This effort even to haul off a sock,
Each night's determined struggle and distress,
Your style becoming more a stumbling block.
To think I thrilled at your once quick unzip,
Cloth's fall and fold come-hither's semaphore;
Strewn lingerie you'd playfully let slip,
Things flung across desire's impatient floor.

How can it be that barely months ago
We fell in all the lust that love allows
And such impediments were passion's charms?
But every move so painful and so slow
As I unbutton carefully your blouse –
A carer still who keeps you in his arms.

18

I dread the days when you hallucinate:
Bad neighbours keep on knocking down our fence.
Your wits no longer can sustain such weight;
A funk, why don't I leap to your defence?
At breakfast time your bolt out of the blue
Of forty faithful years and yet so sure,
Articulate with righteous anger you
Dismiss a guest for being my paramour.

You hear but now can't heed me anymore;
The promised truth I tell your mind's too frail
To grasp; what it rejects it must divert
And all your motives turned to metaphor;
In scrambled dots of dreamlike Braille
I see the signs of your disease. But still I hurt.

19

We so often moved from place to place,
Examined empty rooms and broken showers
And thought how we might share and shape a space
With paintings, books and plants to make it ours.
But now that you, my love, must live in care,
I'm here alone in rooms that I explore;
Yet in my mind's-eye it's too much to bear –
Your face a face along this corridor?

And those misjudgements made along the way,
Mistakes we made reacting to mistakes
Or how we would too hastily decide;
But two maturing even when they stray
Can turn things back around where one heart breaks.
No matter what we'd woken side by side.

20

It's now one week we've left before you leave.
What am I doing doodling time away
In this small world of words and make-believe,
While you prepare your trousseau for the day?
The clothes where laundry tags will soon be sewn,
Mementos, snaps of moments you'll recall;
Already you must make that room your own;
My portrait you want hanging on your wall.

I question all again and agonise.
You've blessed whatever I felt called to do;
Though you may never read these poems I write,
I know you'd never want it otherwise.
All words bear witness to my love for you,
You Bríd, my Beatrice and my Shulamite.

21

Those summer weeks when you had gone away
I waved goodbye but wobbled at my core;
Would time drag on forever and a day?
The doubt of silence as I shut our door.
Your portrait shines your presence like a sign
As though to say 'it's you I'm thinking of ',
That face where sympathy and fun combine,
A woman loved who gave her life for love.

All words too hollow and so beat-about –
Unspoken things are better understood;
Between the safety bars of your cribbed bed
I slide my right arm through, then reaching out
I gently hold your frail and trembling hand.
Our thin but still unravelled crimson thread.

22

An early Friday evening meal with friends;
No drink – too dangerous with medicine –
Your frailty seems so yin and feminine,
The lady host on whom this night depends.

Grace said to bless and thank for friends and foods,
Each guest who shared our table reappears,
All those we wined and welcomed down the years,
Tonight our feasts remembered and renewed.

A deep togetherness, shabbat shalom,
Our party breaks up early as we'd planned;
We're struggling now and helping you to stand,
'I'm tired now,' you repeat, 'please take me home.'

Already left, you're longing to return.

23

Before you leave, like lovers we now creep
Upstairs to use the second floor instead,
Your boudoir and our decades' pleasured bed,
Where cheek by jowl we slept our love-juiced sleep.

A fleeting rendezvous to talk and face
So much we might have done but didn't do,
The gifts I know I should have given you
That you forgive me now in your embrace.

'I know,' you whisper, 'I fulfilled your need,
But if you find a new or younger flame
I wouldn't want you feeling guilt or shame.'
Again you lavish me, my giving Bríd.

While we're alive, I still belong to you.

24

The day of your departure, with a friend
You pack but first you clear a kitchen press –
A spurt of cleaning somehow to express,
This is a new beginning not an end.

Unpacking gear and placing things on shelves
I see you boldly sorting out your clothes;
We've put my portrait on the wall you chose,
Our friend leaves us last moments to ourselves.

Before I shut the door, a final wave,
Then I return to take another kiss;
'O God,' I cry, 'why must it come to this?'
But for your sake you beg me to be brave.

Within your weakness, still the one who's strong.

25

Half-dazed I must have taken some wrong turn.
Detouring home I think I even toyed
With going back, still anxious to avoid
Aloneness I'm reluctant to relearn.

At first I wonder will you settle in.
A cold uprooting, sudden and so strange;
Such chaos now I'm trying to arrange
With plans and flurries of new discipline.

When people ask – although it's genuine –
'How's Bríd?' I bite my lip afraid to cry;
I can no longer look them in the eye
But will myself to hold what wells within.

I wander in a world that's still unreal.

26

This is your house and home as much as mine.
I lie here sleepless in your boudoir bed
Where perfume lingers in our patchwork spread,
And something of your presence seems to shine.

But how must you now feel? I fill with dread.
Another brought by nurses into line?
And yet too young an inmate to resign
To staring at what years may stretch ahead.

Your long-demented neighbours moan and shout.
So frail a mix of body, heart and mind.
A few more weeks and I would fall apart –
Or did I lack in love not holding out?

I toss and do not know which way to turn.

27

My Bríd, who stemmed the bleed of youth's despair,
Without you now I struggle day by day
As busily I keep black dogs at bay
And stick to plans, afraid of laisser-faire.

All files and notes for fear disorder win
And swing from mood to mood and pole to pole;
I summon monk-like years of self-control
To fight a demon gene so deep within.

On top of things and knowing what is what.
But sudden loneness sinks its claws in me;
Forlorn I sob aloud 'Why must this be?'
My God, I cry by day; thou answerest not.

I hold the line alone without your rhyme.

28

We're sitting on a garden's sun-caught seat,
Our weary roles of case and carer shed,
The fuss and stress of pills and falls; instead
As guests and lovers we again can meet.

The need to share an ordinariness
The drive and engine of a passion's dream,
To throb with variations on a theme,
To turn love to love's take-for-grantedness.

Our commonplace now placed in quarantine
And all our meetings seem once more unique;
We thrill at every date although we speak
The language of a lifetime in between.

This peace and ease I know with no one else.

29

I'm lulled a little, think that all is well,
When blusters of despair re-cloud your brain,
A turmoil you no longer can contain:
'Am I to die condemned here in this cell?'

'Is this how I'm to end my earthly days?
I'm left now cooped up in this catacomb;
You signed me in and took my house and home,
Much good to me your tears or poems of praise.'

'O Bríd,' I beg', 'you know that isn't true!'
One side of you it seems must skew and jar,
The other half remembers how thing are;
You shuttle me but you are shuttled too.

You know you're in a dream and yet can't wake.

30

But were our days together just a dream,
A fantasy that slipped so god-damned fast?
Though no love given ever knows a past,
I mourn a oneness sickness can unseam.

I learn to live in this new borderland
Between an innate peace and inner strife;
A woman who has shaped this one man's life,
A stranger I still try to understand.

Had I to choose the null or to-and-fro –
Alzheimer's downward trend without return
Or your returns I have with hurts to earn –
O give me any time your come-and-go!

I pay this price so I can have you back.

31

Before I'd always found you in your room,
Not in the ring around the TV screen;
You'd shunned that circle nursed and overseen,
So daily our old lives for hours resume.

I dread you sitting staring all day long
But cooped up in your small room face to face,
Our closeness hallows that unhomely space,
Together we still know that we belong.

Today I came and found you cribbed in there.
Could this be Bríd? A wounded bird in pain
Whose dignity you're struggling to retain,
Alone and sullen, lost in your despair.

I lean to kiss and claim you with my love.

32

The home's hours measured out by metronome,
The meals and pill times all by rote and rule;
I imagine you a girl at boarding school,
You yearn so much for your first Sunday home.

Disconsolate, you loathe such strict routines.
Once home you cry 'I'm fed up with such fuss,
This is our niche, the nest I made for us –
You do not understand what freedom means.'

If only I could tend you on my own.
I did as much as nerve and bone could do;
But if I fall, who then would fend for you,
Beloved Bríd, so broken and alone,

My boarder held so helpless in my arms.

33

All memories mix longing with relief –
I'm grateful for those years that now have gone
But want that life to still go on and on.
My eyes will waste away with tears of grief.

If I could live my life ten times again,
I'd fall for you the way I fell before;
Would you then choose me ten times more
And make this man the luckiest of men?

At night our house becomes my wailing wall.
In lanterns of recall you still can lope
Across my mind so coiled with spring and hope;
I flood with you anew, my all in all.

How in your wound I love you more and more.

34

All day a woman wails in her distress,
Across the corridor a patient moans;
How do you screen out all the screams and groans,
How can you cope with so much wretchedness?

No wonder you will weave between two poles.
You hear the lives these cries and tears contain,
So praying they can overcome their pain,
No longer heed their grieving rigmaroles.

But then you rage at me. 'Why must I stay?
Why will I not get better. What of bail?
I'm tired of all the inmates in this jail!
And you, you wouldn't last here one wet day!'

Your brokenness cries out. I bow my head.

35

I love the early evening when at ease,
Your spirit debonair and dignified,
We talk or fall to silence side by side
In sacred moments we're allowed to seize

Before the time your mind begins to tire
And flagging you confuse this home with home;
A fraction out of focus hope can roam,
Your brain-fatigue fulfilling your desire.

Then tenderly I tell you where you are;
'O yes,' you smile, 'I'm wandering again.'
But somehow stressed, you frown and strain
To fathom things that seem both near and far.

I know it's best to kiss goodnight and leave.

36

An angry ring at nine to please come now.
I'd just turned in but, worried by your tone,
I'm floundering when you hang up the phone.
What happened? Has there been another row?

I try not run the traffic-lights, although
I speed to find you there still full of rage
That nothing I can say will now assuage;
You've packed and dressed, prepared to go.

In Parkinson's no plan or stratagem –
New outbursts fall outside my scope and skill;
'Those nurses left me nude against my will'
And when I pause, you say I side with *them*!

How can I tend your psyche's unseen wound?

37

You've been so brave. Your pain is still so raw.
This change and move have churned your fragile mind..
I'm told I must be cruel to be kind –
For her to root, I have to now withdraw.

My head says here's advice I ought to heed –
To bring you home delays your bedding in;
All theories demand my thicker skin –
But me pull back from you, my only Bríd?

I know the nurses want you to adjust,
Yet playing fast and loose with you, my love,
By blaming doctors' orders from above
For me would mean betraying all our trust.

I bring you home to board with me once more.

38

Beyond our grief your garden's burgeoning:
Forsythia in bloom, the sun drinks up
Its nectars from each mauve magnolia cup,
This beautiful weekend in footloose spring.

All week I know you wait and how you yearn
To live again those years of life we grieve,
Before the moment when once more you'll leave,
Packed-up to face the pain as you return.

Against advice I'm glad I took the chance.
Two days together. Now the end draws near.
'But how,' you ask, 'will I get out of here?'
Once home I'm haunted by your parting glance.

O Lord, my God, please let this chalice pass.

39

These lines of mine an inner praying must,
My faithful psalms from this new desert land
To make some sense, attempt to understand –
But do these words betray our years of trust?

'You're hanging out our linen stains and all' –
I hear a pressing voice within complain –
'Such poems blurt what should be private pain',
'Our lives become a public punching ball'.

My cries at first seem only self-communed
Unshared half-thoughts that shuttle through my head.
How can I best now weave the crimson thread;
Will someone else find solace in our wound?

My words bear witness to unbroken love.

40

The figures who at first all seemed the same
Are stories you have gathered bit by bit;
By slow discovery's identikit,
Anonymous become a face and name.

The sighing dayroom circle you now brave
With sympathy you summon more and more
For worlds where weakness turns the axle's nave,
Whose axis tracks compassion at your core.

Your presence floods and overflows in me.
Such life enfolded in your lineaments!
I'm awed by beauty all distress accents
To light your face with such fragility.

Here even in your suffering more yourself.

41

No matter what your Parkinson's still mars,
Let everything I do be done for you –
Our trust a word that's infinite and true,
That wills the world around its axle bars.

This poet-guest on whom you can depend,
Your escort every olive garden day,
As I remain your lover come what may –
One crimson thread until the crimson end.

The passion of our years now crossed by pain,
What rose is wound up in the wounded bud
Or marvelled sapphire hidden in the mud?
O Lord, your will not mine this losing gain.

Our love your love that stirs the sun and stars.

42

Good Friday afternoon I come and find
You drooping in a corner on your own,
A dozing migrant in your weary mind;
I weep for you so weak and so alone.

A silent scowl and deep inside I fear
That anger always going on about
How I'm to blame for your now being here;
Your clouded thought begins to close me out.

I am your love life's grieving amputee
Who says I love you as I always do;
Though you no longer add 'I love you too'.
I stoop to steal a kiss that's not for me.

Bereft, I'm leaning on a phantom limb,
My loneliness a ragged broken rhyme.

43

A friend now tells you I am looking tired,
How suddenly I've greyed this month or two;
But you suspect that maybe we've conspired
So that he thinks of me and not of you.

My darling Bríd you can no longer care;
Possessed by Mr P.'s self-centred elf,
Your strange black-mooded eyes just stare
'But he's at home, so he can mind himself.'

You are the one it's best to think about.
My thoughtful spouse what have these drugs now done?
The selfish demon Mr Parkinson
Has turned my real Bríd the wrong side out.

Your psyche somersaults from day to day.
I'm still for you when you can't be for me.

44

In your despair you row and rage at me –
'And you who called my lips a crimson thread
Won't have me home but jail me here instead;
My poet keeps me under lock and key.'

My love, what can I say to comfort you?
You're in no mood to change your wounded mind,
No saying 'now you know that isn't true' –
Such mental links disease has undermined.

I want to tell you I am suffering too –
Without your love I too am so alone.
Can't we enjoy these precious hours we own?
But I can't reach my new and u-turned you.

I start instead embracing your despair
And let my arms say all your mind can't hear.

45

The names you use, the news when we now chat
Seem bulletins from some new boarding school;
Such things you talk of, who said this or that,
The daily drama of monastic rule.

I want to share this theatre too, although
Each time I tap again the locked door's code
And smile goodbye, deep in my bones I know
You're moving in another lore and mode.

Though you upbraid me, you are changing too,
You're learning your own part in this strange play;
New world of lines and cues as day by day
Your life is here. Must I start losing you?

Like you I yearn for then but must choose now.
For your sake too, I'm learning to let go.

46

Why do you so insist I am to blame –
Because for all my care I have no cure?
Or since you know I'll be there all the same,
Despite your damnedest, love will still endure?

You know year in year out that I have seen
How Parkinson's besieged your life by stealth;
Though self-reliant, now you learn to lean
And well you know I know the guilt of health.

'My poet has no pity in his heart.'
No one can wound like you, my muse and wife;
You feel each weakness as you wield the knife.
It can't be you and yet those words still smart.

Although you rage at me I know you know
No angry taunts will taint this love for you.

47

'That lady in the near by room who roars! –
This place is bedlam,' you at first complain.
I want her moved and mention changing floors –
'Remember,' you remind me, 'she is in pain.'

One woman who had washed you was so kind
You felt she had some wound. I wondered why?
It was the way she'd asked you if you'd mind;
You'd seen yourself deep in your carer's eye.

Impulsive love that lingers in between,
An understanding still a part of you,
Some wiring of your nature winning through
For all your agony – that generous gene.

Such glints and glimmers of yourself again,
My giving Bríd that you have always been.

48

Such anger clouds our days of April sun.
O please, my Bríd, I plead again with you,
What would our widowed friends not give for one
Weekend, for even one such rendezvous.

How can I calm this anger's throb and rush
Or stanch your fears, get you to understand
You burn with dreams of birds that flew the bush;
The days we have are still our birds in hand.

Your rage at me a rage at your own rage
Around a bitter ring you can't now break,
Around about the mind's tail-biting snake –
For both our sakes I dare to disengage.

I cobble strategies to help us cope
As I divert you to unloop the loop.

49

Let me drop by your school with some concern,
Re-catch you unawares to watch a while
Until your class shouts 'Micheal!' and you turn,
Your inmost self invested in your smile.

How little then I thought I'd find you here
Asleep in this slouched dayroom mood;
I wait a while, afraid I'll interfere
With flashbacks which your mind like mine has cued.

Despite your grief, such dignity and grace!
Again as in the nights I'd wake and gaze –
Your you-ness overflows my yearning praise;
I stand to stare at this beloved face.

So known and so unknown a nodding shape;
This life that loved and steered me so asleep.

50

The specialist spends time explaining how
A drug you've taken every day for years
Stirs up delusion – even stopping now
Could mean your paranoia disappears.

A wonder that for forty years we're one –
Love bonding biochemical machines –
Yet so much by one drug can be undone,
One tiny daily dosage intervenes?

But could it be that your barrages cease,
Accuser you some weeks ago became,
Believing at long last I'm not to blame?
And would this weaning let you find some peace?

Just one pill less unloop the blaming loop?
I don't know if I even dare to hope.

51

When every day I phone at 8 a.m.
To ask what kind of night you had last night,
I don't know what to think when you condemn
Those carers that you claim are full of spite.

Today recounting how for hours you'd cried
Until a Dutch night-duty nurse came in,
You tell me how in her you could confide –
I'm buoyed up by this morning's bulletin.

That is the woman who once watched me too
As I grew tearful when I turned to leave
And said 'You are doing all that you can do.'
I'm grateful for this blessing though I grieve.

Asleep in guilty sleep at least I know
There's one you trust that watches over you.

52

O let me please, my Bríd, believe my ears
That as I left you said 'I love you too' –
Our life's sweet liturgy for forty years
Until those drugs contrived a double you.

Had I begun to grow a thicker skin,
Though maybe after all I don't need one?
A hallelujah dares to long within –
A day that started dull breaks into sun.

And once again I hope against all hope
That weaned your paranoia now might lift.
Will life allow us this our last-ditch gift?
Without your blame I could I think then cope.

Have I become too careful, too resigned?
I throw my care and caution to the wind.

53

Next day I ride a moody rodeo.
'You're the one who will not set me free!
You're not the man I married years ago –
My sister's right you wanted rid of me!'

I bend to kiss your hunched-ness from above,
To stroke that head that stoops with its own weight;
A ghrá mo chroí thú! Now goodnight, my love –
'Not love,' you snap. 'The word you want is hate!'

That distance I'd intended to maintain,
Then yesterday you filled my glass half-full;
But Mr Parkinson has pulled the wool
And caught me with my guard let down again.

I must stand back to keep such moods at bay,
Then love you more in case you can't love me.

54

Though hardly ever then at loggerheads
We knew that whether we'd agreed or not
We'd never sleep a night on bitter beds
So we'd be morning friends no matter what.

I know things illness says I should ignore
But words are words once spoken which in spite
Of what I know still nag and sting my core.
How can I settle now or sleep tonight?

But must I murder something in my heart
And harden deep within? So here I am
About to sleep though bitter words still smart,
Doze off as if I didn't give a damn.

My Hamlet heart is rocking to and fro.
I veto pain so I'll survive for you.

55

Recalling heydays can for some revive
Delight; for me remembrance still brings pain,
Reminding me and keeping grief alive.
My love, I want to live our life again!

Why should life's music hurt me now too much
As though those things enjoyed somehow conspire,
So two street-lovers' passing glance and touch
Refill me with such unfulfilled desire?

My wounded bird of being singing dumb,
I wake and doggedly begin my day
With discipline I blindly now obey;
How can I say how lonely I've become?

My anguish still an absent paradise;
No loneness like the loneness after bliss.

56

Too soon to dwell too much on memories!
Although things didn't go the way we'd plan,
No life's defined by Parkinson's disease.
Let's bind up both our wounds as best we can.

At weekends we can live a while old lives.
Again you've said 'you are so good to me!'
The thrill of this! You see my spirit thrives
A week on one such moment's eulogy.

Enough the pain and anguish when we part –
These moments we can still both have and hold;
O Lord, renew our days now as of old...
Our cherished time in spite of grief I chart.

What's ours is ours, my love. What's gone is gone.
This bread we break still better now than none.

57

That's how you coped with colds or any ill:
You'd always minimise and underplay;
You never wished it wasn't so – your will
Ignoring it, you knew it went away.

And any time I tried consoling you,
My saying so would only make you worse –
'You cause my shake because you say I do' –
This illness your strong will won't now reverse.

For all your agonies night after night
And days when suddenly you find you freeze,
Again, my Bríd, you're playing down disease –
'Let me come home,' you plead. 'I'll be all right.'

You cry out on your cross of broken will.
Can coping weakness now become your steel?

58

I walk thin ice and watch my step with you –
Our years still thick as thieves but all the same
I'm treading carefully in case that you
Begin again to tell me I'm to blame.

Since slanted rhymes are slightly out of true,
Detach so you'll survive good friends' advice,
But must I fudge or tell a fib or two?
My Bríd, to even think that I'd think twice?

Although you're frail, I learned to think ahead,
Then compensate and catch you if you fall;
So now I try to think before I tread,
Those things that cause you stress I now forestall.

While still afraid to break our sacred bond,
I learn to see the unseen inner wound.

59

This evening when you phone at half-past nine
And weeping want to know why I won't come,
I'm torn and don't know where to draw the line;
My head says no, my heart wants to succumb.

I know your mind's fatigued, how you're afraid
And in distress your phone's the straw you clutch.
You'd look for more however long I stayed
And in the morning not remember much.

'I'm tired,' I plead, 'about to go to bed' –
'You won't come though you're just three miles away?'
'But Bríd, it's late, please settle down,' I say –
Yet can't believe I say what I have said.

To hold the line or let my own life slip?
I turn and turn and sob myself to sleep.

60

But damn you, Mr Parkinson, you sneak!
You've thieved the mellow stage we thought we'd share;
I mourn these ripened years we meant to reap,
The autumn of our lifelong love-affair.

The greatest grief that even grief must end?
I'm trying to transcend this agony;
Despite myself, for your sake I intend
To live once more the life you shaped for me.

Because of you I am what I became –
You wouldn't want me dour or woebegone?
I hope I have the verve to carry on,
But grief concealed is grieving all the same.

Again I'll joke and laugh, begin to heal;
Can pain and laughter travel parallel?

61

I've set you as a seal upon my heart –
Creation aims beyond its winding down –
Our passion's raging flame, death's counterpart
That neither waters quench nor floods can drown.

Despite Gethsemane I still will bless
Our lightening poem bolted from the blue,
A cosmos summoned out of nothingness,
This promised world of meaning made with you.

Of course desires or dreams and yet beside
This gift of love all else just foam and fizz;
Our long and never-broken trust, my bride,
Still taps the sap of all that always is.

We loved up love that rhymes so perfectly;
One crimson thread all through eternity.

62

We're visiting a kind psychologist
As geriatrists juggle medicines;
No luddite, I salute both disciplines,
Yet is there a dimension they have missed?
Unknown to you some lack is nagging me;
Of course drugs tweak our chemical machines
And kind psychologists adjust routines –
Will no one nurse your spirit's agony?
Beyond the drugs or easy dreams of cure
A reckless suffering both plumbs and primes
The depths that yearn in you, beloved Bríd,
For meaning in what you now must endure.
I turn to my priest friend from schoolboy times
To tell me who could tend your spirit's need.

63

He'll mull it over for a month or two,
Approach a woman in the interim
Who once in illness had watched over him;
A favour for a friend, she'll walk with you.
Are there some things you cannot say to me
But need another to confide in now?
Are our two lives so close they can't allow
You word deep secrets of Gethsemane?
Though years of medicines had zonked your mind,
Psychosis wastes and you're more self-aware.
What broke the spell that overcast your brain –
A tended soul or drugs or both combined?
I'll never know, my love, and I don't care;
I only know that you are you again.

64

Again you're you and yet your choice is stark:
More dopamine might let you move about,
But at what price? The doctors have no doubt –
More medicine would sink your mind in dark.
Such elegance each morning since we met
And how I loved to watch the way you dressed;
Although you can't now cope you're still distressed
To find your life so deep in others' debt.
'What good am I to God or man?' you cry.
We have what Mr P. can't undermine,
Our years of hand in glove still not ungloved;
I pleat my hand in yours as I reply:
'Be you, my love, the you who's always mine;
You're beautiful as long as you are loved.'

65

On Saturdays and Sundays coming home
To live again our old lives side by side,
I sense that you too sense, my guesting bride,
The tick and nod of our love's metronome.
So tired by six you pack up to return;
Uncomplainingly you take your bedlam place.
I bow to kiss you, keeping up a face,
As parents leave a pupil they intern.
At sing-alongs or simple-simon quiz,
Just one companion, someone sound of mind?
The carers here are kind, it's not their fault.
But now that you again are you is this
The best of all the bedlams I can find?
Alone outside I cry my tears of salt.

66

The wise soul-friend who tends you week by week
Has counselled rest, serenity and space,
Another nursing home. She names a place
Where she once helped and knows it is unique.
'The Blind Asylum' we said growing up,
The school for sightless girls that since became
A nest for ailing women, the halt and lame.
I've talked with you, determined to apply,
But mum's the word. We have to wait and see.
Five minutes' walk from home, from door to door!
Does waiting mean to wait for one to die?
No cure. More light and more serenity.
I dampen down our hopes in case they soar.

67

Today though weak you went to see the place
But wheeled around it must all seem unreal;
To wait for word another strange ordeal –
We'll keep our secret dark still just in case.
I went this evening, walked again the grounds,
Around the cut-stone church and convent wall.
But could this be your final port of call?
Would things be easier in these surrounds?
How often on warm evenings we'd half-heard
Ave, Ave, ring out from somewhere near'
Its aftermath to evening angelus
Still wanting all *according to thy word*,
Yet never knew the angel tolled from here.
And will this summoning bell now sound for us?

68

I came back late and caught you by surprise,
All dignity and understated style,
But seeing me again your sudden smile
That seems less on your lips than in your eyes.
Those deepening eyes that know me through and through
Now shine between a twinkle and a grief
At this disease, your sly life-sapping thief –
And yet such heartache keeps enhancing you.
In spite of pain, more lovely day by day
In your fragility; it seems I too
Must grow to room this grandeur at your core.
Love's womb I thought so full again makes way.
Completeness still completes itself in you
And every time we meet I love you more.

69

Just now word came that we have got a place.
I'm glad yet anxious that our answered prayer
Means someone moved to more intensive care;
For you this change a challenge you must face.
It's over seven months you've soldiered here;
I wonder will you miss the known routine
Or find such new surroundings too serene,
Secluded in that cloistered atmosphere.
Good Cora who's in charge of care thinks best
We hush all till the move. And right away
As internees scoop tunnels towards a dream,
You'll pack now, practical and self-possessed,
So bag by bag I'll smuggle things each day.
Our shaft of hope is shovelled towards its gleam.

70

How every Sunday night outside I'd grieve,
Aware how no one was of sound mind here,
No table-mate or possible compeer –
We'll pass a last time through this door and leave.
All ringed around the dayroom's blaring screen,
Yet still those soaring moments when they'd sung
A Strauss-like waltz *One day when we were young*
And women crooned for how things once had been.

For all the noise, a caring catacomb
Where tongue-tied migrants tended with such heart,
Caressed non compos mentis clientele;
Despite my grief I'm grateful for this home
And watch with wonder as you now depart
How carers kiss and hug a fond farewell.

71

Your room that's even bigger than we'd thought
Looks on a lawn. Delighted with the view
We sort what clothes and gear you've brought;
Once more I hang my portrait here for you.
Friend Emer eager as last time to brace
Us both is busy now advising this or that;
The one thing we all three keep wondering at,
These lavish courtyards full of light and space.
Such hope glows through stained glass above the stairs
To hallow this once convent's generous hall;
As white light prises rainbows from a prism
I'm warmed by Joseph's coat till unawares
That first farewell I can't but help recall
Re-salts the wound of our unwanted schism.

72

You take your courage in both trembling hands.
I think of how a young girl you'd moved schools,
New names and faces with new lists of rules;
My Bríd, again you're braving fresh demands.
But will it take you weeks to settle in?
Our hopes for here so soon fulfilled in spades –
You name three understanding stalwart aids,
Your Christine, Alison and Catherine.
Re-rooting now we both must realise
This haven well could be your final berth;
Yet I believe each time I leave you're safe.
So ripe with humour, patient, worldly-wise,
Three Dublin women gently down-to-earth
All watching over you, my darling waif.

73

You're stiff from sitting still so long a time,
But moving slowly find yourself dismayed;
However even with your walking aid
Your spirit's still a sprinter in your prime.
Though tired, your walk a kind of cautious plod,
We take a turn around a court with care
And make it down the corridor to where
An oratory cores the tiny quad.
Through glass we glimpse an older nun who bends
In prayer that's magnified a thousandfold;
Her stillness, all our caring's counterpart,
Sustains a peace on which this home depends;
While sisters pray, the centre still will hold.
We must not fear that things will fall apart.

74

How wonderful those drifted friends that we'd
Known once so well who gladly now return,
Re-knotting severed nodes in their concern,
And those we knew less well turned friends in need.
I understand some stall or balk at grief,
While meaning well from week to week delay,
Or busy ones who simply fall away –
But yet large-heartedness beyond belief.
What would we do without our staunchest friends,
Our Emer, Paula, Oliver, Corinne,
Who each has grown through grief they learned to bear,
And met while minding you? Their love transcends
All falls to tend our tightrope's unforeseen;
We're carried in the meshwork of their care.

75

Around half-eight I rang you just to say
I love you – deep in me you've never left;
I hear a voice so rueful, so bereft:
'But am I getting home again today?'
How at the start you'd managed with a stick,
Then worsening would need a walking aid
And now your chair. But frail and so afraid?
Your question's tone has cut me to the quick.
But me decide for you one-sidedly?
In all our years that never was the way.
How could that be the calm and steady voice
Which always lavished hope and heartened me!
Of course, my Bríd, you're coming home today.
We're still together and I still rejoice.

76

On weekend mornings wheeling you to mass,
Each ageing nun a rustling chaperone
Caressing you like light from coloured glass;
In this belonging warmth we're not alone.
Bright Mary Duffy, sightless since age six,
Is led to read the Sunday psalm in Braille –
Your ways, O Lord, are love – the blind and frail
Embracing in Christ's name their crucifix.
This home become our new community,
I'm Sister Mary's Sunday baritone
Half-humming hymns I know from childhood days;
Then sings my soul, my saviour God to thee –
Blind years of worship sound these walls of stone.
Is all our suffering subsumed in praise?

77

Today as now for fifteen months my day
Turned on the axis of its afternoon;
Once more short hours of honeymoon,
Our being side by side, not what we say.
I'm tuned in unison and share with you
So much that in our silence we assume
The rambling ease of memory's living room
Where no one else can know me as you do.
Although I yearn to visit you again –
Just like last night – I'm never certain how
I'd raise false hopes of nightly rendezvous.
But if you weren't there, I'd rue it then.
I love you in this heartache here and now.
In every choice I make I choose for you.

78

Tonight I came and found you holding court –
Three friends at once but caring for each one;
You're busy asking after Paula's son,
Supporting all who come to give support.
You broach a joke but now you're breaking up
So we just laugh at your infectious laugh;
A hostess pouring out her heart's carafe,
You're topping up your callers' loving cup.
Life hasn't taken such a turn; believe
We're entertaining Friday evening friends –
Again you're tending guests, my table queen,
We've never thought how Mr P. will thieve
Togetherness; my giddy love pretends
I'm glancing all as it has always been.

79

This Sunday as another season veers
You sit in silence while I tend to food;
It seems you're soaking up your garden's mood
When suddenly I see you've filled with tears.
O no, there not the years that we'd dreamt of.
'I'm sad,' you say, 'that I have failed you now.'
I hush you in my arms to tell you how
This suffering still sounds our depths of love.
A lusty green, your first and pliant growth –
That it can be you've grown more beautiful
Now crimson surges in the sumac's leaf?
I think such beauty grows in seeing both
The verdure's push, the autumn's vivid pull.
I feed on gratitude in spite of grief.

80

You tell me how in sleep you turn to me –
Alone I talk to you into thin air;
The instant when the other isn't there,
Our uncurbed need for things that can not be.
From here two buildings block your home from sight.
I think how children played with thread and tins,
Made telephones to thrill their bulletins
From house to house clandestinely by night.
O still I know the moments when you stir;
Asleep I sense your every toss and sob
And turn to reach you in our tenured bed.
As though close-woven even thoughts transfer,
Your yearnings cry for years of joy that throb
Across one love's unwaning crimson thread.

81

Dementia? But you're so sound of mind?
I dare to think the doctors got it wrong;
That dopamine and mimic drugs combined
Misled their diagnosis all along.
Those months confused, ignoring my concern,
For no good reason you could cut up rough;
I never thought then that you might return –
My God how can I give you thanks enough?
We never come to time, it comes to us.
O moment when the mango kisses lime!
Our every moment now a moment plus
And this I'm telling you is double time.
But even wishes wished our life outdares,
This resurrection way beyond my prayers.

82

Each afternoon our catch-up tête-à-tête.
A pattern forms as weeks and month now pass;
It's twice a week our in-house dining date,
At weekends we come home here after Mass.
Those wainscot corridors, the hallway dome
Where helpers, nuns and nurses greet by name;
I start to feel at home when in that home –
A déjà vu so different yet the same.
The chapel, quads and double swinging doors,
A waft of kitchen smells and stainless steel,
Refectory mealtimes, linoleum floors –
A monk in me can yield to their appeal.
As once we both were shaped by boarding school,
We're roosting in our new monastic rule.

83

I seem to celebrate on your account,
Today so rigid under my caress.
I kneel to kiss you now but no amount
Of love or care can lessen your distress.
Clear-mindedness but no more dopamine,
So you're chair-bound, can barely move alone;
An unoiled body's messaging machine
Shows all the drugs had blurred is now full-blown.
At least this deal allows the mind to mesh
And yet I know that you must pay the price;
Your Mr P. will have his pound of flesh
And this trade-off means such a sacrifice.
What can I do to settle suffering's bill
Except to say, my Bríd, I hold you still?

84

So precious now this weekend afternoon
When side by side we face a garden's mood;
In silent moments now we commune,
The said and unsaid of our lives collude.
The light makes leaves a flickered honeycomb
As, yielding to its fall's first yellowings,
A silver birch we bought and ferried home
Engraves our loving years of growth in rings.
I take you on a tour of garden plants;
Advising this be trimmed and that replaced
You deal with each like one-time confidants,
Some brushed aside and others re-embraced.
In you your father feels a garden wall.
I see him cutting briars before his fall.

85

'You won't mind, will you?' you are asking me,
'I'd like to give this necklace to a niece' –
'Of course I don't,' I say and yet I see
Another letting-go, a new release.
These native amber beads I bought for you
One autumn in Chicago you had kept
Among your things, as though you always knew
All gifts are loans we fleetingly accept.
I loved the silver links and thick black thread,
The oblong beads intense and warm to touch
And strung like decades stretching out ahead –
Those many years have given us so much.
The glory of our gift this amber's glow;
Are both of us now learning to let go?

86

Around your table there is room for four.
For fear of fire, the carers must replan –
The mobile move up to the second floor –
You miss your neighbour Mary Corrigan.
I've gone back in again this afternoon
And heard your table talk begun anew;
At first I know she'd seek out help but soon
By touch and tap she makes her way to you.
At nineteen sightless, sixty years she's here;
Self-taught by tapes a reflexologist
Until her stroke, blind tending volunteer.
She says she'll go – 'No stay, please,' I insist.
Such care just coming. There's no fret or fuss.
Soft-spoken courage calms and heartens us.

87

How bravely day to day you seem to face
The creeping power of Mr P. the thief;
Then breaking down you sob in my embrace,
Your fragile chassis shaking in its grief.
When you begin to weep, the selfsame way
The fullness of your laugh infected me,
My matching heart is moved by your dismay
And soon I start to cry in sympathy.
'I never thought our time would end like this –
I'd planned to visit every place with you' –
Imagining the travels you'll now miss
You name the things you once had thought we'd do.
Your soul and body both dissolve in tears
As all your being mourns imagined years.

88

Our lives had slowly woven into one;
School classmates' names you mention filter through –
Hortance and Joan and Anne – so I'd begun
To feel I shared those boarding years with you.
One time you showed me windows in one wing
Where once your bed and cubicle had been;
Through glass I glimpse as I come hurrying
Three women known that I had never seen.
From days of ribbons, prizes, schoolgirl pranks,
They've come again to comfort you, my Bríd;
I meet your Mary Haughey and May Shanks,
Your Maura Harkins heartening you in need.
In silenced dorms what did you dream of then?
Four lived-in lives here catching up again.

89

Some afternoons there are 'activities'
When most are wheeled or struggling make their way
For crosswords or some other grey-cell grease
That keeps the mind and memory in play.
You tell me how you have to take great care
And not outdo the resident dab hand;
Though ninety-five, she's watchful and aware,
A champion determined to withstand.
It's you still young, the swiftest in your school,
Whom some humility keeps holding back
For fear you'd hurt; your heart must overrule
The will to win, the ego's cul-de-sac.
What good to gain a world and lose a soul?
This love again keeps holding up the whole.

90

In Sunday's falling light we sit and talk,
Amazed as always, almost at a loss
To say how we are blessed. To think your walk
Of life and mine might easily not cross!
Yet neither you nor I quite fit the norm
And maybe links in our genetic map,
A streak in both refusing to conform,
Allowed once distant orbits overlap.
Our plotted lines defying any plan,
What were the odds that we should ever meet?
Against the laws of chance we two began
Our livelong pillow talk on Parnell Street.
Some hand would have us meet by hook or crook,
By luck, by guess, by gift, by love's own fluke.

91

Arriving early here to take you home,
I find Lorraine still fastening up your blouse;
'Now Bríd,' she coaxes you, 'where is your comb?'
I wait for you as your spectator spouse
And watch this woman as she daughters you
To tend your matchstick frame's fragility;
But blessing all she does, out of the blue
A wave of loss is welling up in me.
Though grateful, grief keeps seeping through again,
The ooze and sting of anguish at my core;
A tenderness my heart's room can't contain
Still wants to love you even more than more.
Such freight of spasms your body has defrayed.
I see how frail you are. I am afraid.

92

You ask for photo albums you took care
To store and now from time to time you thumb
Through faces of unfearing youths who stare,
All courage, innocent of what's to come.
Our one and only wedding photograph,
Your kerchief simple yet so debonaire;
But midis and those platforms, 'Look!' you laugh,
'Your trousers flared and you're so trendy there!'
A blurred remembrance stirs in each tableau
As, leafing through our decades face by face,
You're leaving things behind and letting go –
My bride I lift again in my embrace.
And then a cry you'd throttled all day through:
'O I'm not ready yet to part from you.'

93

You tell me your return on Sunday night
In all the week is still the worst you know;
I see again a young girl lithe and slight,
A yearning boarder sixty years ago
Who gazes still at Errigal that looms
Between both Ballyconnell House and home.
One boom-town building here now screens your room's
Prospect from me, one business superdome.
Your bag, your phone, your bell – small ministerings
That slowly settle you. Then heart-on-sleeve
We swap in whispers our sweet everythings.
So many times I seem to make to leave
But linger still. As lovers in their prime,
We turn again to kiss just one more time.

94

The angel of the Lord declared – you'd led
Again this half-forgotten midday prayer,
When good Assumpta with her silent tread
Comes giving off her upright girl-like air.
She smiles and sees your needs, however small.
Another sister tells she's eighty-nine –
A carer who makes daily calls on all;
I watch the way her ageless face can shine.
Flower-lovers both and lavishers of care –
Plants you get as gifts Assumpta tends
And waters; in her visits' warmth I share
Your suffering's unreckoned dividends.
The word made acts of care and water poured;
Indeed *behold the handmaid of the Lord.*

95

We telephone our nightly bulletins,
About when they're undressing you for bed;
As children talked with spools and polish tins,
We throb across our unseen crimson thread.
Tonight you're weary, so your voice is weak –
You'd quite a deal of visitors today –
And yet your tone and timbre, though you speak
So low, means I decipher all you say.
That Kasha kissed you when she left on leave –
Such gifts and surplus outside our control –
My giving lover's learning to receive,
As caring women care beyond their role.
I think how love responds to love alone.
'Good night,' we murmur on a mobile phone.

96

Alone I've ordered my whole life just so,
A place for all and everything in place;
Together we'd gone gently with the flow,
Both safe and sabbathed, in our embrace.
Gone now the nightly tugged-for double sheet,
Our bits and pieces strewn in heat or haste;
I know like me you know it's all too neat,
Our life's accoutrements too coldly placed.
But there's some feel to things you satisfy
On Sundays reconnoitring your terrain,
When straining, stretched out on our bed we lie
In one another's arms this once again.
My routines mourn the messiness of two;
A sweeter mayhem in me yearns for you.

97

You pick red beads you got from Singapore
And tell me they're the keepsake kept for me;
You know I love that necklace that you wore
The day you sat for painter Mick O'Dea.
My darling red, your favoured royal blue,
The colour of the blouse you want to wear
Laid out; but less a realist than you,
Such down-to-earthness I'm not sure I dare.
We cannot plan who's first to go, I plead,
But lack of daring blinks at your ordeal;
So many signs I need to hear and heed.
'Does no one know,' you ask, 'how tired I feel?'
And either way a farewell both must face.
I fold you in another fond embrace.

98

In my half-monkhood now I seem to spend
My mornings in my inner overdrive
Or tackling household things I need to tend –
A day's work done the time that I arrive.
I find these precious hours when we confide
Our daily blow-by-blow accounts instead
Of sitting gently by your armchair side;
I like to chat here lounging on your bed.
But no! And have I drowsed again? God knows
Each time I fight a while the falling sap
Before despite myself I fail and doze.
I came to be with you and yet I nap
And lie here mellow in your aspen's lee.
So tremblingly your love keeps watch for me.

99

I'm told to plan to take a break away,
A fortnight, I explain, to fill the tank;
At once you start to urge a three-week stay,
But near the time I noticed your heart sank.
I know the days before I left had gnawed
A worried bone: 'Who'll be my next of kin
'If I should breathe my last while you're abroad,
Then will they know which blouse to wake me in?'
By mobile every morning when I wake
I'm sounding out your form; the same reply
As always, though I'm sure I hear your shake –
You answer first by asking how am I.
I know, my bride, that now your mind's your own,
Your body does not have a selfish bone.

100

These moments we both live in high relief.
Your calm we took for granted has become
A gratitude scaled up in joy and grief;
Where once you'd curbed your tears, you now succumb.
Such understanding under such thin skin;
Although you'd been the one who'd empathise,
Now others' sorrows surface from within
And fellow feeling wells up in your eyes.
But look! you're watching rooks that wheeled and whirled,
Before they roost and risk once more to soar
And sail across your window on the world.
I've never seen your face so bright before.
We trust the passing angel's silent tread,
Our love still one inwoven crimson thread.

101

One Friday at your lunch you seemed to fret
And tell me how so easily you tire;
Again I say 'I love you, don't forget
That you are always all I could desire.'
I stay till two and when I start to leave,
'I'll miss you now,' you add, surprising me;
I wait a half-hour more as though to thieve
Unknowingly one last epiphany.
Of course I'll call around once more tonight
To catch you unawares or half-awake,
So you'll look up and beam in your delight
A smile that you've been saving for my sake.
I dither somewhat turning out the door
I blow a kiss, then face the corridor.

102

Our roofer rang to say he was delayed –
I had, it seems, forgotten he was due!
Though I've come home I half-wish I had stayed.
To share this news, I find I'm phoning you.
'Just since you left I've been unwell,' you say,
'I'm lying here, just hold on now a bit';
I'm listening to the silence of delay
Where every second seems it's infinite.
A sudden sound. A rattling breath as though....
I phone you back at once, then phone the home.
Please get to Bríd! But should I wait or go?
Each moment ticks its silent metronome
And minutes lapse into delirium.
The dreaded call-back says 'You'd better come.'

103

O Lord, I cry, remove this cup from me,
Don't take my bride, as running out of breath
I'm forced to walk the wainscot gallery.
But must 'you'd better come' mean only death?
On turning down your corridor I meet
A shock of nurses, carers and a nun
Lined up. I understand – no need to greet –
Just silent hugs from carer Alison.
Did someone say I think your Bríd is gone?
Inside your room the sounds of urgent men
Resuscitating your oblivion,
Then word they have your heartbeat back again.
Your spirit leaps within its envelope;
I'm hanging by a crimson thread of hope.

104

You're eking out your life in A and E,
Wired up and piped and waiting here in queue
For scans to scrutinise your brain to see
The damage done, how best to tend to you.
While nurses harbour you behind their screens
I fumble numbers on my mobile phone,
Speak shakily on answering machines;
Your lover still I sit and hope alone.
But Joe a Jesuit and friend has come
And, reaching down to underwrite your need,
With chrism he gently signs Christ's cross by thumb
On your unknowing brow, my darling Bríd.
Then one by one friends come to watch with me
In this dark garden of Gethsemane.

105

We're told they've moved you to intensive care –
I traipse past trolleys with recoverers
Who feed my anxious hope, and find you there
Among the bleeps and pulsing monitors.
Here one to one a nurse is watching you;
They're chilling you so body changes slow –
Though damage done they cannot now undo,
It's kept in check by cold adagio.
My love, to lean on time's sweet I.O.U.,
I hold your frozen hand and try to pray.
What are the chances that you'll now pull through?
Until reheated it's too soon to say.
It may be Monday when they'll really know.
O God, you hold me in your touch and go.

106

The night nurse notes a steady graphing screen
As lateness tumbles over long-dayed June;
He'll phone if there is something unforeseen,
I'd best go home, come back again at noon.
I nourish old sweet nothings in your ear –
O yes and yes, I'm still here right nearby;
Then taking heart I ask 'If you can hear,
Just lift a lid, my Bríd, and blink your eye.'
It's much too soon and so I have to wait,
Content my mumbling tone has reached to you;
I know that in this cold you hibernate
And my soft nothings still are *entre nous*.
The nurse adjusts one blipping dial a notch;
Reluctantly I leave my bedside watch.

107

Once home, so heavy-eyed I'm overcome
With sleep that mothers me an hour or two;
I wake and think I hear machines that hum
As night nurse William watches over you.
My sleeplessness a numb, demanding ache:
Must I now set your suffering spirit free
Or is it all a nightmare? Will I wake
To have you here again alongside me?
Will I still be the lover by your bed
Or left a lonely widower behind?
Why does this heartbreak racing on ahead
Keep forming varied futures in my mind?
I toss and turn in storms of broken thought;
Imagining tomorrow I'm distraught.

108

My heart can never have enough of you.
All Sunday as I sit and wait I know
Deep down the doctors see what I see too;
It's hours until we have to let you go.
You'd lain too long and that impaired your brain;
They can't undo the damage you've sustained;
No sign of purpose or a hint of pain
To indicate a consciousness regained.
Sedation down, they'd thought you might improve;
They watch but you're completely unaware –
By now at least a lid should maybe move –
But, just in case, another day in care.
I yearn for signs. I flood remembered years.
You seem to move in my mirage of tears.

109

At 4 a.m. the startling telephone –
There's been a change, better I am there.
I've promised not to let you die alone,
Though no one knows how much you're now aware.
Ten minutes and I'm sitting at your bed,
A sudden fever raised your heartbeat's rate;
The summons might have meant that you were dead –
Relieved, I hold your hand again and wait.
I'm told there's nothing now to do until
The doctors can consult and then decide;
Here murmuring how much I love you still,
My voice is keeping vigil by your side.
So long a love, so one in flesh and bone;
My Bríd, this is my touch, this is my tone.

110

I meet a kind bad-tiding medico,
Am told this afternoon what I had known:
They'll stop the ventilator, let you go.
Should I be left to say farewell alone?
I pause a moment. Is this parting mine?
Or is your death an opportunity
To let in you so many intertwine?
You're hostess to a whole community.
My one request: I'm waiting on my friend,
Who's flying in to be here by my side;
Of course, they say, they can delay the end
Until I tell them – I myself decide.
To die alone, my love, has been your dread;
A roomful gathers now around your bed.

111

A priest anoints you, binds us all in prayer.
I stroke your brow and bending from above
Am startled by your sudden flickered stare –
I snatch up your last fleeting act of love.
The crimson moment cries for you, my bride,
Yet I'm so glad that I have caught your eye;
You've seen me here and know I'm by your side,
I'm grateful for the gift of your goodbye.
Between us two so little left unsaid –
But one last kiss, my sweet viaticum
As softly switches click behind your head;
You breathe each shallowed breath till you succumb.
And we who weep and hug are newly bound;
Unless a grain of wheat fall to the ground....

112

The last two years I've watched as you prepared
This crimson moment, gathered memories in,
As we rehearsed a hallowed lifetime shared –
I should have no regrets and no chagrin.
You're viewing faces in a photograph
Where you, my love, are still so swift and lithe,
Or standing in your garden with your staff –
I see your father falling with his scythe.
Each afternoon your aspen elegance
Held court for all who came as best you could;
Envisioning my sorrow in advance,
You hosted friendships for my widowerhood.
This faithful circle sealed by death you leave.
O God, I am so grateful; yet I grieve.

113

For forty-four sweet years all thoughts were swapped.
Alone I'd list things in my mind to tell;
Will you now shape the tone I should adopt,
Your guessed response my ghosting sentinel?
I know you will and yet I wish for more:
I want to hear your words, your gentle tone
Caressing me with reasons as before;
I yearn for you anew in flesh and bone.
But everywhere your spirit's overspill –
I name you and once more you are so near;
Your presence wraps its care around me still,
As if your going leaves your love more here.
I must depend on wisdom you impart
In take-for-granted habits of my heart.

114

For two years now each night I know how you
In care would keep your grace and dignity
By choosing fresh ensembles, something new –
No matter what, you still delighted me.
But you'd reminded me so recently
Where your assigned blue blouse and black suit were –
So careful you'd be stylish cap-à-pie,
A beret picked to lend a bouncy air.
By some mistake the undertakers made
Your cap is plopped too carelessly on you;
I saw how you now seemed quite disarrayed,
Returned to set it tastefully askew.
All chosen well and nothing left to chance,
You woo our God of joy with elegance.

115

Returning to St Mary's one more night
Will let both friends and carers take their leave;
The solace of a final touch or sight
For those who've grown so fond of you they grieve.
You're for the church this evening – Father Joe
Has gone ahead to greet you – men begin
To let us know that now we need to go;
The time is come, my love, to lid you in.
Unseen your pencil skirt must hug your hips,
Yet still some black sets off your royal blue;
I lean again to kiss your balmed-up lips
And gaze again to fill my eyes with you.
I stared to store your face as best I could,
To hoard the lineaments I love for good.

116

O no, I'll never be an elegist
And you won't slip into my yesterday;
So I still say I kiss and not I kissed,
And keep to present tense communiqués.
I want no mourning or past tense laments;
I don't now shower you because you died
With rosy-coloured hindsight compliments –
God knows I'm proud I praised you on this side.
One lover and all things to this one man –
Such joy you'd kept incarnate and so fresh
Those almost forty-four sweet years we span.
We speak in spirit all we spoke in flesh.
The past and present hover in suspense;
We live our lives now in this double tense.

117

My friend who homaged you and your career
Saw two rich threads inwoven through your life:
A teacher tending with delight each year;
A woman, lover, hostess, muse and wife.
Your gift for giving wove two strands to one,
Till Mr P. had turned the tables round;
Then carers did for you all you had done
So willingly before those strands unwound.
And yet you gave in your attentiveness
As others' cares became your own concern,
So those around you shared in care's caress
Where we are all both weak and strong in turn,
That sudden smile as listening eyes engage;
To love was still your call at every stage.

118

O Bríd, all branches of your lifetime came,
From Dublin years, from childhood Donegal;
Some thankful pupils, peers, an older flame,
All now returning for your curtain call.
Those close a while who drifted or withdrew –
From all our phases faces reappear
And come to honour and to hallow you,
Or help to brace your broken sonneteer.
Our Cora came from where you first had gone
And Philomena from your final berth,
Archille and Aylish, Anne and Alison
Farewelling you before you went to earth.
Your absent reap and gathering still astound;
Wheat grain that's fallen fruiting in the ground.

119

Your nephew Séamus read from Song of Songs
And who is leaning there against her love?
My Shulamite, a bare-boned shoulder longs
To take your weight. I am your one-winged dove
Who's here, my Bríd, and trying to be brave,
Although I tear each time I hear your name –
I grieve a passion fiercer than the grave,
Its darts are darts of fire, a raging flame....
Awake, o south wind, come north wind,
My bride, my honeycomb, my confidante –
By every turn and twist our lives were twinned
In Solomon's blue-curtained covenant.
You set me as a seal upon your heart.
But must my Shulamite and I now part?

120

Your godchild's reading of psalm one-two-one
Kept ringing in my ears as we arrived
Into Shanganagh's mid-June midday sun
To bury you, the woman I once wived.
Together we decided we'd lie here,
Consort between the mountains and the sea;
It's like Gaoth Dobhair though somewhat less severe,
And not so far from our biography.
They dug the deepest grave I ever saw
To house your gentle spirit's earthen jar;
So long a hollow lowering to its maw –
My two thrown crimson roses fell so far.
I must now trust to God's slow grinding mills.
My love, *I lift mine eyes unto the hills.*

121

How you and I so nearly never met.
Imagine if I'd missed that one small ad
Or hadn't looked and found that flat to let,
Which soon became our love life's launching pad.
The landlady's fire hung, she'd half said no;
'You wouldn't want a man to live above,'
She'd urged a lady in the flat below;
To think she nearly had bud-nipped our love!
Supposing you'd opposed this tenant man
And she'd refused to sign and do the deal,
I wouldn't have this lifelong gift you gave.
Where others had left off your love began;
Upon your arm, my bride, *you set my seal*
As firm as death and fiercer than this grave.

122

This pain could break me, I could fall apart;
Yet for your sake intent on walking tall,
From years of happiness still taking heart,
I am determined gratitude is all.
Our hoarded memories my second sight,
As parted now our lives still parallel
And move in silent lines of shared delight;
I honour you in wanting to live well.
But grief sneaks up in spite of gratitude –
A bracelet found I hadn't seen before
That floods my tears; a flashback now and then
Which breaks my heart. Although I do not brood,
So much I've had, so much I want you more;
My memories still mourn for all again.

123

The thought your mind might fail so hard to face,
You'd always worked to keep your brain awake;
I'd read aloud *a language and a race*,
'It's African', I add – we give and take –
'No, five; begins with *b* and ends with *u*' –
Me looking at the words, you working blind;
I'd watched the way you'd crack a crossword clue,
Amazed that you could hold it in your mind.
Our memories seem halved in our long haul,
So what I'd jumble you could join again
To solve some biographic anagram;
Things bandied back and forth that we'd recall,
Our thoughts like hemispheres cohered one brain.
And who'll now know that half of who I am?

124

I splice my life that now seems split between
The ones who knew you, those who'll know of you;
Your exit, love, a curtained end of scene –
A fallen veil divides my world in two.
One half I know can reminisce with me
And share the face these love-poems still enfold,
Or recognise in me a memory
Of you who shaped the shape I try to hold.
The other half will know by hint and trace
How in your love all roles could coalesce;
A wooer, temptress, lover, muse and wife;
In passion's lines or in your portrait-face,
By hearsay or by gazing some may guess
The life we lived before this afterlife.

125

Would someone come who'd understand my sort
And match me inch for inch with mind and heart?
Before all failed, had somehow fallen short;
I'd yearned for you, my only counterpart.
By formula still far too young to yield,
Should take my time in making up my mind,
And playing fast and loose first play the field,
Keep thriving on the chase more than the find.
Now looking back how little I then knew –
Imagine if I'd gone and let you go?
So proud you'd chosen me to be your man,
Though young I saw what I had found in you;
At least I knew, my bride, enough to know
You'd love with all the love we humans can.

126

Still letters keep on coming every day;
So many missed the notice, didn't know,
But now that word has reached them write to say
They understand what I must undergo.
And then how they remember you, my Bríd:
The smiled concern, so gentle and sincere,
Your grace, your laugh; though grateful as I read,
The sobs I thought I'd mastered mutineer.
I know how proud I was in praising you,
Your thoughtfulness, your understated style,
Yet never sure what friends had really known;
And now I see how much all others knew –
O yes! But passion smouldered in your smile;
How fiercely you could love I know alone.

127

You once had said you were too old for me.
'O please,' I'd pleaded, 'do not jilt me now,
We've fallen for each other fancy-free,
Why should we heed convention anyhow?'
You knew deep down what your huge love would dare,
Although if asked our age you'd acted coy;
With years, of course, when learning not to care,
You'd joked about your growing bonnie boy.
I'd struggled with a shake, was highly strung;
But you redeem your trembling troubadour
As in the ripened blur of years roles blend.
Yet you, my aspen mistress, still were young,
Your suffering spirit sparkled even more –
For all your ailment, ageless to the end.

128

I know you'd danced and dated with the best,
Young flirts and flings of spontaneity;
What did I do or what had so impressed?
Why in the world should you just wait for me?
In conversations names came up again –
Did you know why they didn't fit the bill?
Almost half-casually you could explain:
This one too secretive, that one too still.
Look who you found to fellow you in bed!
Well, certainly not still or secretive
But praising loudly you I'm so proud of;
Before you'd gone I'd asked you to forgive
My lacks. 'Our life was wonderful,' you said.
Were all my faults and flaws transformed by love?

129

This warmest weather started as you left;
Your garden, Bríd, runs riot in the sun
As ground weeds climb through every flagstone cleft,
Our roses swell in summer's overrun
Of plantains, mallow, bindweed, bittersweet –
A world so lush that I refuse to weep;
You're present still as evenings hold their heat
And it's so hot that I can hardly sleep.
How unawares my undermind delights!
As fingers fit and work a puppet's glove
My dreams replenish every pleasure zone
And live old lives of hot midsummer nights,
Embraced in memories of making love.
All warm with you, I wake again alone.

130

Invited now to visit by my friends,
Although I'm thankful, I will still remain
To spend time where our spirits co-extend,
And lie here where for decades we have lain.
For if I roam I fear that, once paroled,
I'd put life off, postpone the calendar;
Though keeping half reality on hold,
I'd wind up with my days the way they are.
But steadied by your presence here instead,
I let your reigning spirit chaperone
My dreams, which now must be both old and new.
I work and lead one half the life we led;
I cry when I still need to cry alone.
You're implicated in all things I do.

131

Your journeys ended June the twentieth,
A dozen days before our marriage date;
The Monday morning I record your death,
One day before we're due to celebrate.
But we'll commemorate – though we're apart –
That lovely white and lime-green that you wore;
Your matching kerchief so demurely smart
Still captivates a memory's encore.
'You'll need a marriage cert,' clerks put me right,
Then ask the date and knuckle down to spell,
Yet do not stop to think this is the eve.
I want to nudge them, tell them how that night
Our friends had called on us to wish us well;
But silently I fold our cert and leave.

132

Your Walkman's there among the things I take,
Its dial still geared to Gaeltacht radio;
Through restless nights you'd lie there wide awake,
Tuned to a life you'd lived incognito.
So small a gadget smuggling words to you
That echo childhood's take-for-granted tone;
I'm thankful this receiver helped you through
A sleepless spell or mornings spent alone.
I see you sitting in your corner chair,
Au fait with all the news of world affairs,
Yet rooted still in parish push and shove;
No show or noise, but sure of who you were,
You bear a world to which we both are heirs;
You're listening to the language of our love.

133

You'd smile coquettishly and cock a brow –
Enjoying what so many might find strange,
As twinkingly you'd liked to tell me how
In different tongues my character could change.
Unthreatened, you had wanted me to thrive,
To travel still my mind's plasticity,
Where old and newer me's in turn connive;
Your love would both rebind and set me free.
You understood the newer self I'd need,
Another nurtured personality,
A part of me that sought its counterpart;
Then I'd come back reborn to you, my Bríd,
Who'd house and home this other different me
Within one lavish many-mansioned heart.

134

How did the like of you, my love, appear?
Serene and radiant in all you wore,
A jaunty-scarfed and gentle pioneer,
My Isadora Duncan of Gaoth Dobhair.
Where did your freer spirit spring out from,
So quietly different and unorthodox;
Less cutting loose than courteous aplomb,
That shuns convention and yet never shocks?
What noiseless daring in your dance of genes
Evoked your nature, summoned you by name?
What chance or grace combined in how you grew
Through choices made among your might-have-beens
Once mixed and matched the person you became,
This once-off woman I have known as you?

135

I grieve among old photographs of you
To choose which best recharge our span of years;
Together it was now and always new,
I settle solo memories' arrears.
I love the searching Mona Lisa eyes
The studio photographer had faced;
The sheen and shade of you that mesmerise
Me still, your halter-style so subtly spaced.
Although those eyes had startled from the start,
I didn't know, my love, how they would lead
To those seen in your portrait's second-sight;
Your story kept the start and end apart.
The novel your life wrote I now reread,
My heroine moves in love's double light.

136

But when I walk alone I miss you most.
Bare-shouldered I now pass at my own pace
The twosomes sidling by and so engrossed
In their attention to each other's face.
The courting couples in their novicehood —
All dawdle-dazzle in delirium —
Still startled someone else has understood,
They blink into the blitz of what's to come.
I bless them as I bless the long-lived pairs
Both joined and shaped by love's assured routine
Till likeness sometimes lapses into quiet,
Their ease shared cadences of joys and cares;
The murmurs of our words that might have been
A silent riff heard in their ripe delight.

137

As I had pledged, I've kept my discipline,
Determined to hold firm and dignified;
But, Bríd, this thieving grief again breaks in
And oozes through me tears I thought had dried.
My head and heart say gratitude is all.
How many know the happiness we had?
Alive I praised you. Why this wailing wall?
My love, my love, on slopes of Gilead.
Yet everything conspires to spill my tears:
Puccini snatched by chance as Madam pined,
Or when my memory for seconds dims
And thinks another's you until she nears;
A body overrides its balanced mind,
Your loss is lodged covertly in my limbs.

138

I keep prayer lists of friends alive and gone,
A ledger I've divided by a line,
Two columns of my networks counted on,
An open mesh, the gauze of what is mine.
And you, my Bríd, who'd topped the living list,
You're still my woman, still my once-off bride;
Though I'm your love's reluctant elegist,
And you have moved across that vague divide.
How are you still so much a part of me?
You're not just absent though I know you've died,
But like our other steadfast friends, instead
We all now merge in one community
Where love can stretch its span, at ease astride
A line between God's living and God's dead.

139

I will refuse to mope or woo despair;
Each morning still, no matter what, I work;
A daily stint, another daring prayer –
For you I must not lose my shape or shirk.
I need the slog and sweat, the nag and drive,
The grace and grind of self-forgetfulness;
For all my grief, as long as I'm alive,
This sense of awe, a world I want to bless.
Contours I start to shape my steadyings,
My work's a ballast and a counterweight;
Unless I graft, my line is out of true.
I strive to find the hidden form of things;
These moods of life I recapitulate
My only honest means to honour you.

140

A friend encouraged and accompanies me –
It is so hard to say too soon or not –
Again I'm in Shanganagh cemetery,
Come back to stand here by your burial plot.
I've found grave 57 A13,
A Buckley and a Farrell neighbours now;
O Bríd, I'll touch the broken Nazarene,
I trust the hem but don't know when or how.
For weeks your presence felt intensified,
But here is where your frame and housing are;
The limbs of such a limber body rest
That once embraced me as my July bride,
Your bones that store the traces of a star,
This envelope of you my love caressed.

141

O I know you're there in all I dare to do,
The way I think and everything I write;
As if in absence you are yet more you
And still my muse, my silent second sight.
How you're inscribed discreetly in small ways;
The teapot and the towels you picked in red,
The place I choose to put the china vase,
And see! I sleep still this side of our bed.
Though you are near and I am not alone,
These poems poured for you are none the less
My Chinese whispers through a Chinese wall.
I long for you, my love, in flesh and bone;
I want to hold, to hug and to caress
The one for whom I meant the most of all.

142

You went before you even were aware.
Despite your spirit still I know to go
Like that was probably your secret prayer;
All tell me how it was a blessing so.
You'd read the books and knew each stage you'd reach
And knew what Mr P. had still in store;
How swallowing can go, the slurring speech,
And you'd become dependent more and more.
Imagine if your mind had been impaired,
With all your horror of that drift downhill,
If knowing and unknowingly you'd slid –
Just look how much your spirit has been spared.
My head thinks this, my heart is struggling still
To say it's best you went the way you did.

143

I'm somewhat steadier and dare some days
Abroad with friends. Afraid I'll come too late,
I make my way through Dublin airport's maze
And park myself near my departure gate.
I find I'm reaching for my phone to say
One last goodbye and tell you that I'll be
In touch a little later on today.
Yes footloose now but I'm not fancy-free.
Though keen to travel mastering all I could
And play the language-loving acrobat;
We knew each trip would deepen and renew
Our startled love. I'd never understood
That talk of being free from this or that;
My freedom was my being free for you.

144

How wonderful to laugh again, unwind,
Enjoy with friends their joy and warm goodwill;
And yet my loneness seems so underlined,
My sense that I am flying solo still.
I'd always liked to look for something small,
A tactile sign of love's conspiracy,
An Isadora scarf, a Danish shawl,
But mostly rings or costume jewellery.
A turquoise nuggets toggle necklace bought,
A set of amber beads, an agate ring –
The fun of finding what would just suit you.
More than the thing itself you loved the thought,
And wore at once whatever gift I'd bring;
'I love you' echoed in 'I love you too'.

145

I'm not quite sure if I now should be glad
Before the pain of grieving's pitch and toss
I'd practised keeping house alone and had
My long and slow apprenticeship to loss.
In care more than two years before you fell,
It seems as though, so I would be bereft
In stages, you had staggered your farewell
And somehow love had planned the way you left.
Phase one had lasted long enough to see
That stunned by loss I didn't start to bask
In sultry moments of despair, and mope;
Although so often you'd permitted me
To dream away some dreaded household task,
You knew at least that I had learned to cope.

146

This morning my Collected has arrived –
Again the minx of grief ambushes me –
How, Bríd, you'd celebrate if you'd survived
And savour this first handling ceremony.
Just days before you died when proofs had come,
You'd longed to do what you had always done,
But couldn't; you'd no choice but to succumb,
Let others proof books you'd proofed one by one.
I lift this yield of forty years of thought,
Whose cargo weighs at least a kilogram,
And open it this first time on my own.
In everything I wrote you are inwrought,
And now your name my *in memoriam*.
I hold our two lives in my hands alone.

147

Alone with hindsight I'm recalling how
So soon at your insistence that I swore
Myself to silence and under such a vow
You'd told me what you'd never told before.
You told me once you'd hesitated, yet
No game of 'I love you, I love you not';
Your indecision needed me to set
Your mind at rest – I'd love no matter what.
That secret care I'll carry to our grave –
But wavering, unwittingly you'd prime
A tenderness, a hidden undertone;
So from the start our love's a standing wave
Whose amplitude was fixed and firm through time.
I know now that your heart had always known.

148

How must I now imagine you, my Bríd?
I stared with love before they lidded you;
But will that still-life image soon recede,
Re-quickened in that naked face I knew?
Always open-countenanced you'd kept
On changing; which of these to choose to see?
A slew of you's with whom for years I'd slept
And woken crowd my wounded memory.
But slowly now each memory matures.
My silk-scarfed Isadora of Gaoth Dobhair,
You merge with Beatrice and the Shulamite,
Then re-emerge to smile the smile that's yours,
As dancing paradise's disco floor
You're swaying lithely towards some dazzling light.

149

My love, I'm still here in the midst of life;
Though I don't stray from you it seems so strange
That in the daily riff of things so rife
With chance, I find that I must slowly change.
My grief is learning yet how you must be
Now less my mate and more an inner coach
Who keeps on breathing memories in me,
What we have shared still shaping my approach.
My core is full of you as I recall
We'd asked if one of us were left alone
How best we both would thrive. My Bríd, I throw
Life's dice – God knows where it may dare to fall.
In all of what's to come no comfort zone;
I only know *I don't know how to know.*

150

The warmest summer we have had for years,
September too has eked warmth day by day;
Yet grief still lurks collecting its arrears –
The pain of loss the price of love we pay.
A cord of covenant until the end.
Awake o north wind and wake south wind...
You were so long my lover and best friend.
One would be first to go; a twin untwinned.
And even as you dance eternally
The faithful arms of memory enfold
You, Bríd, in yellows, browns and beads of red,
In shades and hues of autumn's sumac tree.
My beloved's mine and I am his to hold
A whole life through, our love's one crimson thread.

MIX
Paper from
responsible sources
FSC® C007785